Printing Practice 1st Grade:

Easy Learning Fun for Kids

Speedy Publishing LLC
40 E. Main St. #1156
Newark, DE 19711
www.speedypublishing.com

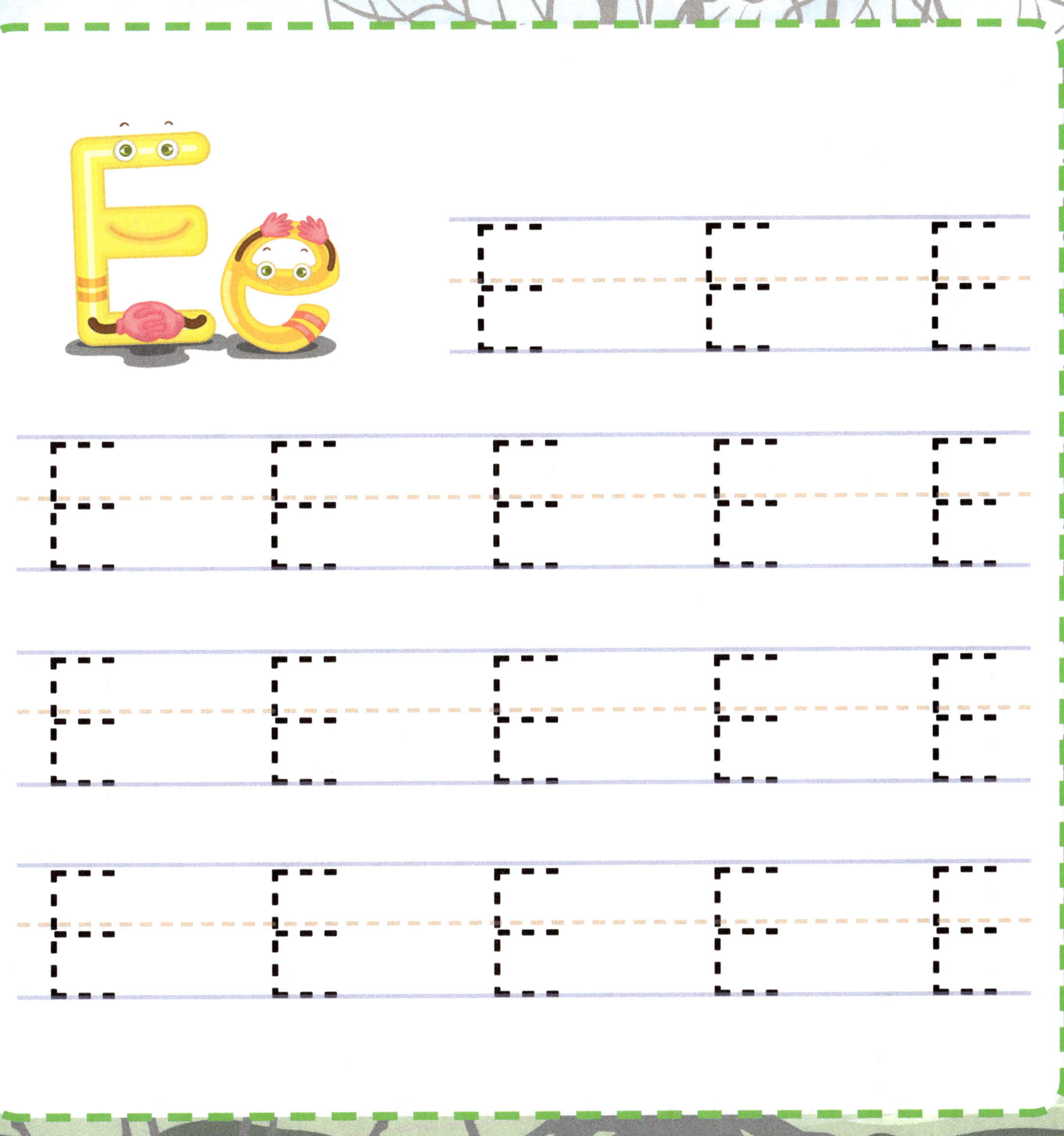

L l

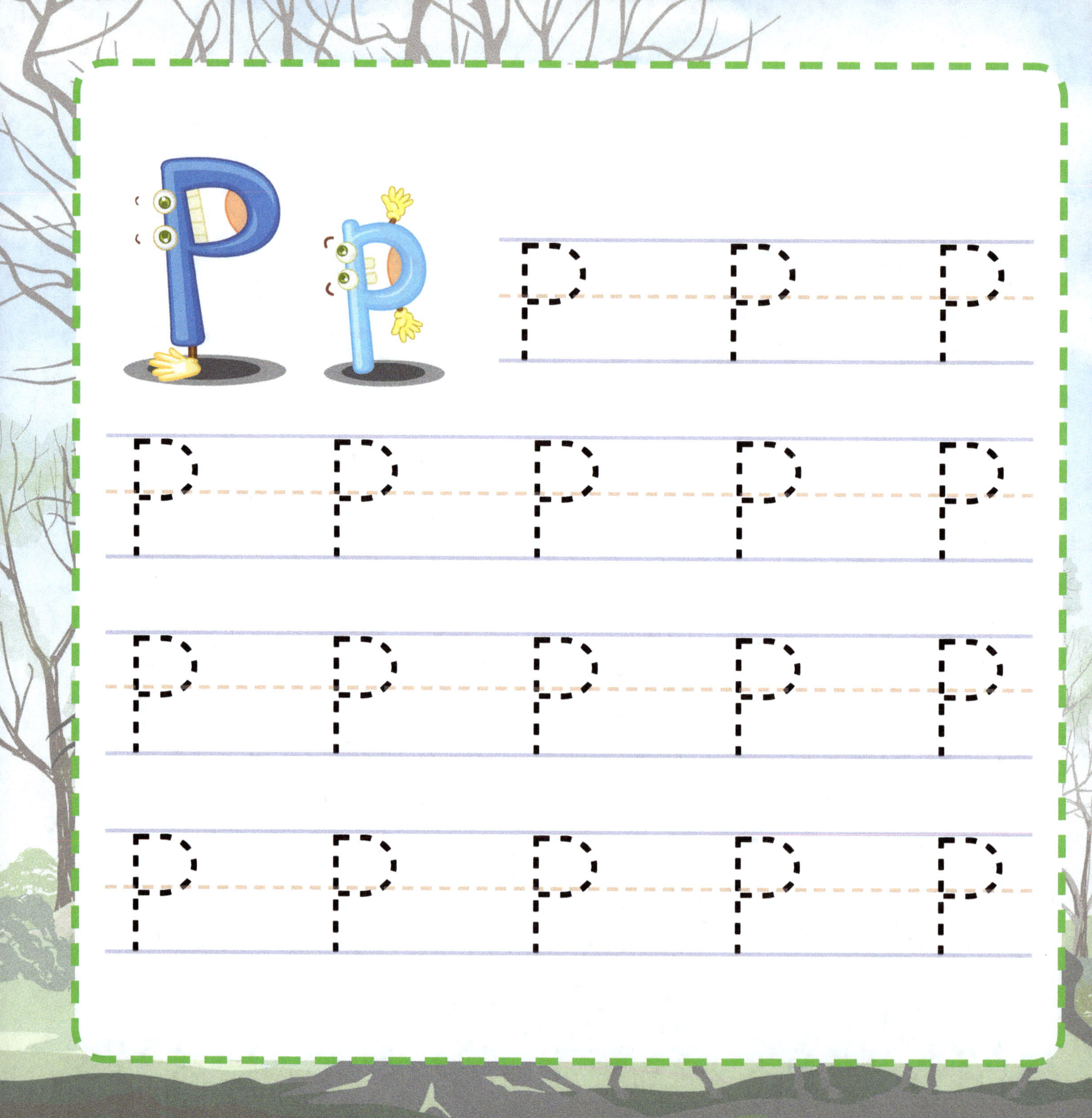

a a a a a

a a a a a

b b b b b

b b b b b

g g g g g

g g g g g

h h h h h

h h h h h

m m m m m
m m m m m
n n n n n
n n n n n

u u u u u
u u u u u
v v v v v
v v v v v

Trace the letters.

Aa Bb Cc

Aa Bb Cc

Now do it on your own.

Trace the letters.

Dd Ee Ff

Dd Ee Ff

Now do it on your own.

Trace the letters.

Gg Hh Ii Jj

Gg Hh Ii Jj

Now do it on your own.

Trace the letters.

Kk Ll Mm

Kk Ll Mm

Now do it on your own.

Trace the letters.

Nn Oo Pp

Nn Oo Pp

Now do it on your own.

Trace the letters.

Qq Rr Ss
Qq Rr Ss

Now do it on your own.

Trace the letters.

Tt Uu Vv Ww

Tt Uu Vv Ww

Now do it on your own.

Trace the letters.

X x Y y Z z

X x Y y Z z

Now do it on your own.

www.ingramcontent.com/pod-product-compliance
Lightning Source LLC
LaVergne TN
LVHW060830170826
845678LV00010B/1941

* 9 7 9 8 8 6 9 4 5 5 6 3 5 *